BILL AND HILLARY CLINTON

AMERICA'S FIRST COUPLE

JEFF MAPUA

Britannica®
Educational Publishing

IN ASSOCIATION WITH

ROSEN
EDUCATIONAL SERVICES

Published in 2015 by Britannica Educational Publishing (a trademark of Encyclopædia Britannica, Inc.) in association with The Rosen Publishing Group, Inc.
29 East 21st Street, New York, NY 10010

Distributed exclusively by Rosen Publishing.
To see additional Britannica Educational Publishing titles, go to rosenpublishing.com.

First Edition

<u>Britannica Educational Publishing</u>
J.E. Luebering: Director, Core Reference Group
Anthony L. Green: Editor, Compton's by Britannica

<u>Rosen Publishing</u>
Hope Lourie Killcoyne: Executive Editor
John Murphy: Editor
Nelson Sá: Art Director
Nicole Russo: Designer
Cindy Reiman: Photography Manager
Amy Feinberg: Photo Researcher

Cataloging-in-Publication Data

Mapua, Jeff.
Bill and Hillary Clinton: America's first couple/Jeff Mapua.—First edition.
        pages cm.—(Making a difference: leaders who are changing the world)
Includes bibliographical references and index.
ISBN 978-1-62275-425-0 (library bound)—ISBN 978-1-62275-427-4 (pbk.)—
ISBN 978-1-62275-428-1 (6-pack)
1. Clinton, Bill, 1946–Juvenile literature. 2. Clinton, Hillary Rodham—Juvenile literature.
3. Presidents—United States—Biography—Juvenile literature. 4. Presidents' spouses—United States—Biography—Juvenile literature. 5. United States—Politics and government—1993-2001—Juvenile literature. I. Title.
E886.M28 2014
973.929092'2—dc23
[B]

                                                                                2014001219

Manufactured in the United States of America

CONTENTS

INTROD

President Bill Clinton and former secretary of state Hillary Clinton have taken turns supporting each other as they ran for different political offices.

I n 1992, the world was changing in major ways. The Cold War, the period of tension that existed between the United States and the Soviet Union, was coming to an end. Now that the Soviet Union was broken up into several smaller nations, the United States remained as the only superpower in the world.

In addition to this global transformation, important changes were also taking place in the United States. The Republican Party had won every presidential election since 1976. This streak ended when a Democrat won in 1992. Governor William Jefferson ("Bill") Clinton of Arkansas was elected the forty-second president of the United States. A popular president, Clinton oversaw the country's longest peacetime economic expansion.

President Clinton and his wife, Hillary Rodham Clinton, became household names. Unlike many First Ladies before her, Hillary Clinton took an active role in politics. While in Arkansas, she worked on programs that aided children and the disadvantaged and maintained a successful law practice. During President Clinton's presidential campaign, Hillary greeted voters, gave speeches, and was one of his chief advisers. In 1999, Hillary launched her candidacy for a U.S. Senate seat representing the state of New York, where the Clintons had moved following the end of Bill's presidency. Eventually, Hillary would become a presidential hopeful and the secretary of state under President Barack Obama.

William Jefferson Blythe III was born on August 19, 1946, in Hope, Arkansas, a small town near the Texas-Oklahoma border. His father, a traveling salesman, died in a car crash three months before Bill was born. A few years later his mother, Virginia Dell Blythe, married Roger Clinton. He moved the family to Hot Springs, Arkansas. An alcoholic, Roger sometimes beat Virginia; the two divorced but then remarried. As a gesture to help hold the family together, Bill eventually took his stepfather's name.

BILL'S EARLY INTEREST IN POLITICS

Bill Clinton became interested in politics at an early age. In high school, he traveled to Washington, D.C., as a senator of the American Legion Boys Nation. There, he met President John F. Kennedy, an encounter that solidified his political ambitions.

Clinton attended Georgetown University in Washington, D.C., earning a bachelor's degree in international studies in 1968. During his junior and senior years, he worked for Democratic senator J. William Fulbright of Arkansas, chairman of the Senate Foreign Relations Committee, whom Clinton later called his mentor. Fulbright was an outspoken

President John F. Kennedy shakes hands with future president Bill Clinton in 1963.

QUICK FACT

President Clinton plays the saxophone and once considered becoming a professional musician.

critic of the Vietnam War, and Clinton opposed the war as well. He received a draft deferment for the first year of his studies as a Rhodes scholar at the University of Oxford in England in 1968. He later attempted to extend the deferment by applying to the Army Reserve Officers Training Corps (ROTC) at the University of Arkansas Law School. He soon changed his plans and returned to Oxford, thus making himself eligible for the draft, but he was not chosen.

HILLARY'S EVOLVING POLITICS

Hillary Diane Rodham was born on October 26, 1947, in Chicago, Illinois. She and her two younger brothers grew up in Park Ridge, a Chicago suburb. Her parents, Hugh and Dorothy Rodham, were a business owner and a homemaker, respectively. Hillary went to public schools. Influenced by her parents, she was a Republican in her youth. As a teenager, she joined the Young Republicans and was active in the First United Methodist Church.

In 1965, Hillary went to Wellesley College in Massachusetts. Her political views changed while she studied political science, and she became a Democrat. She began to support the civil rights movement, women's rights, and protests against the Vietnam War. She soon joined the Democratic Party. In 1969, she graduated with a degree in political science.

Hillary went on to Yale Law School. There she developed a strong interest in family law and issues affecting children. She earned her law degree in 1973.

QUICK FACT

Hillary says that in junior high, she wrote to NASA inquiring about entering into the space program but was told they didn't take women.

THE CLINTONS ENTER PUBLIC LIFE

In 1970, Clinton entered Yale Law School. While there, he met Hillary Rodham. Together they worked for George McGovern's presidential campaign during the summer and fall of 1972. The following year, they both graduated from law school. Clinton returned to Arkansas to teach at the University of Arkansas School of Law, while Rodham briefly went to Washington, where she worked for the House of Representatives staff during the

Before they became one of the most influential couples in politics, Bill and Hillary were just two of many law students at Yale.

impeachment of President Richard Nixon. She
also stayed in the East to work for the Children's
Defense Fund. In 1974, Rodham moved to
Arkansas, where she taught at the University of
Arkansas School of Law. She married Clinton in
1975 and joined a prominent law firm in Little
Rock, later becoming a partner. The couple's
only child, Chelsea, was born in 1980.

Bill's first political campaign, for a seat in
the U.S. House of Representatives in 1974, was
unsuccessful. However, the close race brought
Clinton statewide attention, and two years later
he was elected attorney general of Arkansas. In
1978, he won the governorship. At age thirty-two,
he was the youngest person to be elected
governor of any state since 1938.

Clinton lost his bid for reelection in 1980,
but he regained the governor's office two years
later. (Until 1986, the term of office for Arkansas
governors was two years.) He was reelected
three more times by substantial margins. A
centrist Democrat, Clinton made educational
reform and economic growth top priorities of his
administration. His educational improvements
included increased spending for schools,
expanded opportunities for gifted children,

and advancements in vocational education. He also raised teachers' salaries and introduced the country's first program to test teacher competency. To encourage investment in the state, he granted tax breaks to industries. He also introduced one of the country's first workfare programs, which required welfare recipients to do some work for the money they were given.

Clinton became a prominent member of the Democratic Leadership Council, a group that sought to move the party's agenda closer to the center of American politics. A 1991 poll of governors named him the most effective governor in the country.

While Clinton served as governor of Arkansas (1978–80, 1982–90), Rodham worked on programs that aided children and the disadvantaged, and she maintained a successful law practice. Her decision to keep her maiden name, however, brought criticism from some traditionalists. In 1982, she began calling herself Hillary Rodham Clinton.

THE PRESIDENCY

Clinton announced his candidacy for president in 1991. His campaign was nearly sunk by

■ Bill Clinton *(right)* and Al Gore celebrate winning the Democratic nomination for president and vice president at the 1992 Democratic Convention at Madison Square Garden.

charges of marital infidelity that were published in tabloid newspapers. He was also accused of unethical conduct in legally avoiding the draft during the Vietnam War. He survived, however, to make a strong second-place finish in the New Hampshire primary. Clinton secured the Democratic nomination in June 1992. He chose Tennessee senator Al Gore as his vice presidential running mate.

QUICK FACT

U.S. citizens do not directly elect their leaders. Their votes actually elect the 538 members of a group called the electoral college. These electoral college representatives, in turn, cast votes for the presidential candidates.

Facing incumbent President George H.W. Bush, Clinton argued that twelve years of Republican leadership had led to political and economic stagnation. He expressed sympathy for the concerns of ordinary Americans, emphasizing such issues as jobs and health care. His personal warmth and charisma, coupled with his moderate views, helped him to defeat Bush and independent candidate Ross Perot in November 1992. Clinton captured 43 percent of the popular vote to 37 percent for Bush and 19 percent for Perot. Clinton defeated Bush in the Electoral College by a vote of 370 to 168.

CHAPTER 2

LEADERS OF THE FREE WORLD

Bill Clinton's presidency got off to a shaky start. His attempt to fulfill a campaign promise to end discrimination against gays and lesbians in the military was met with criticism from conservatives and some military leaders. In response, Clinton proposed a compromise policy—summed up by the phrase "Don't ask, don't tell"—that failed to satisfy supporters of either side of the issue. His first two nominees for attorney general withdrew their names because of ethics questions raised against them. Republicans in the Senate blocked two major pieces of legislation—an economic stimulus package and a campaign finance reform bill. Clinton would have to work hard to make the changes he wanted to see.

FIGHTING FOR WOMEN

Despite these early hiccups, Bill Clinton's first term had many successes. He changed the face of the federal government

Bill Clinton's cabinet included women and minorities such as Madeleine Albright, Jesse Brown, and Federico Peña.

by appointing women and minorities
to important posts throughout his
administration. Among them were Janet Reno
as attorney general, Donna Shalala as secretary
of Health and Human Services, Joycelyn Elders
as surgeon general, Madeleine Albright as
the first woman secretary of state, and Ruth

Bader Ginsburg as the second woman justice on the U.S. Supreme Court. His wife, however, found that many people were not ready for a politically active First Lady.

With a professional career unequaled by any previous presidential candidate's wife, Hillary Clinton was heavily criticized. Conservatives complained that she had her own agenda because she had worked for some liberal causes. During one campaign stop, she defended herself from such criticism by asserting that she could have "stayed home and baked cookies." This impromptu remark was picked up by the press and used by her critics as evidence of her lack of respect for women who are full-time homemakers.

QUICK FACT

Al Gore gained even greater renown after the vice presidency for his environmental work and his book and related documentary on global warming, titled *An Inconvenient Truth*.

FIGHTING FOR HEALTH CARE

During the 1992 campaign, Bill Clinton sometimes spoke of his close partnership with Hillary as a "twofer" ("two for the price of one") presidency, implying that Hillary would play an important role in his administration. Early signs from the Clinton White House supported

In 1993, Hillary Clinton fought to reform health care in America.

this idea. She appointed an experienced staff and set up her own office in the West Wing, an unprecedented move for a First Lady.

Clinton appointed Hillary to head the Task Force on National Health Care, a centerpiece of his legislative agenda. Her job was to help devise a national health care policy. The plan included providing health insurance to every American. She encountered criticism when she closed the sessions of the task force to the public. Doctors and other health care professionals objected that she was not a "government official" and had no right to bar them from the proceedings. An appeals court later supported her stand, ruling that presidents' wives have a long-standing "tradition of public service" acting "as advisers and personal representatives of their husbands."

To promote the findings of the health care task force, Hillary appeared before five congressional committees. She received considerable and mostly favorable press coverage for her expertise on the subject. But Congress ultimately rejected the task force's recommendations. Hillary's role in the health care debate galvanized conservatives and helped Republicans recapture Congress in the 1994 elections.

NAFTA AND HELP AT HOME

The North American Free Trade Agreement (NAFTA) is a treaty that promised to create a common market in North America by dropping trade barriers between Canada, Mexico, and the United States. President George H. W. Bush, Canadian prime minister Brian Mulroney, and Mexican president Carlos Salinas de Gotari signed

Ahead of the 1996 election, Bill Clinton delivers a speech about American workers.

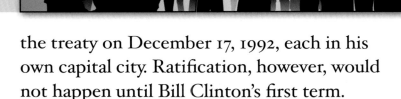

QUICK FACT

In international law, an agreement that is binding on two or more nations is called a treaty.

the treaty on December 17, 1992, each in his own capital city. Ratification, however, would not happen until Bill Clinton's first term.

Though Clinton supported it, the treaty was opposed by many in Congress and most labor unions. Environmentalists also opposed NAFTA because of lax enforcement of environmental standards in Mexico. However, state governors overwhelmingly supported the treaty because of increased trade and production potential for the states. In 1993 Congress passed the trade agreement, which went into effect in January 1994.

In 1996, Clinton, building on the welfare reforms he had implemented as governor of Arkansas, approved legislation dismantling the sixty-one-year-old national welfare system. He declared that the legislation provided a "historic chance to try to recreate the nation's social bargain with the poor." The bill, which split the Democratic Party, ended the federal guarantee to the poor that was established in the New Deal era of President Franklin D. Roosevelt. The new measure handed federal money to the states to run their own welfare programs, with the stipulation that no family stay on public aid more than five years and that able-bodied adults work within two years of receiving benefits.

During Bill Clinton's first term, Congress also enacted a deficit reduction package and some thirty major bills related to education, crime prevention, the environment, and women and family issues. Among them were the Family and Medical Leave Act and the Brady Handgun Violence Prevention Act.

Terrorism and Foreign Policy

The United States was targeted by terrorists several times during the Clinton years. International terrorists bombed the World Trade Center in New York City (1993), the U.S. embassies in Kenya and Tanzania (1998), and a U.S. Navy ship in Yemen (2000).

In foreign policy, Clinton inherited from the Bush administration military commitments to United Nations peacekeeping missions in Somalia. He withdrew U.S. forces from Somalia, a country torn apart by clan fighting, after much public pressure.

Bill Clinton took a leading role in the ongoing attempt to resolve the dispute between Palestinians and Israelis in the Middle East. In 1993, he invited Israeli prime minister Yitzhak Rabin and Palestinian leader Yasir Arafat to Washington to sign a historic agreement on Palestinian self-rule. In 1994, a U.S. peace delegation successfully negotiated the return to power of Haiti's democratically elected president, Jean-Bertrand Aristide, who had been ousted by a military coup in 1991.

CHAPTER 3

The end of Bill Clinton's first term provided challenges overseas. He and Hillary had made changes in the United States, and now they could make a difference around the world. With strong leadership, the Clintons would be able to earn a second term in the White House.

CLINTON AS PEACEMAKER

In 1991, the Balkan nation of Yugoslavia was torn apart by civil war between opposing ethnic groups. Ethnic Serbs, who opposed the breakup of Serb-dominated Yugoslavia, launched armed struggles to carve out separate Serb-controlled territories in the breakaway republics of Croatia and Bosnia and Herzegovina (which were once part of Yugoslavia but had declared their autonomy). The Serb separatists were given military support by Slobodan Milošević, leader of the Republic of Serbia. They systematically attacked other ethnic communities, murdered

U.S. peacekeeping troops salute President Clinton on a trip to the former Yugoslav republic in 1996.

many civilians, and sent others to concentration camps.

After Croatian troops trained by retired military personnel turned the tide against the Serbs, President Clinton took advantage of the momentum and introduced a framework for peace. A conference began on November 1, 1995, to find an agreement among the leaders. A peace agreement, called the Dayton Accords, was reached on November 21, 1995, by the presidents of Bosnia, Croatia, and Serbia. It ended the war in Bosnia and outlined a General Framework Agreement for Peace in

Bosnia and Herzegovina. Peace has lasted since the signing of the Dayton Accords.

Strong Economic Growth

Clinton's reelection in 1996 had much to do with the country's strong economic performance during his first term. The economy continued to grow throughout his second term, eventually setting a record for the nation's longest peacetime economic expansion. By 1998, the Clinton administration oversaw the first balanced budget since 1969 and the largest budget surpluses in the country's history.

By the end of his second term, Bill Clinton would oversee the creation of twenty-two lower number of teen pregnancies.

IMPEACHMENT

Following accusations of an improper relationship with a White House intern, in late 1998 President Clinton was impeached (accused of misconduct in office) by a grand jury on charges of perjury (lying under oath) and obstruction of justice. He was subsequently acquitted (cleared of wrongdoing) by the U.S. Senate. Despite his impeachment, Clinton would leave office with the highest approval rating of any U.S. president since World War II.

PUTTING FAMILY FIRST

During her husband's second term as president, Hillary continued to travel the world in support of various causes. For example, she met with leaders overseas about human rights. However, throughout her career, Hillary Clinton always put a priority on taking care of children. She continued this trend in 1997 by helping United States senators Ted Kennedy and Orrin Hatch pass the State Children's Health Insurance Program (SCHIP). The program was a federal initiative that provided state support for children whose parents were unable to afford health coverage. In addition to SCHIP, Hillary also pushed for immunizations against childhood illnesses.

The 1993 report pictured was given to the First Lady by the American Bar Association as part of her support of American families.

QUICK FACT

Immunizations, or vaccines, protect individuals from dangerous, and sometimes deadly, diseases.

For older citizens, Hillary chose to address the health issue of breast cancer by encouraging older women to use their Medicare coverage to receive mammograms. A mammogram is a procedure that uses special X-rays to produce images of the soft tissues of the breast. It is used to investigate breast lumps and screen women for breast cancer. Continuing to push for better health, Hillary increased funding for research into prostate cancer, the leading form of cancer among men in the United States.

Hillary Clinton had a longtime interest in helping children with special needs find homes and improving foster care programs. There were disagreements over what should be done, but Hillary led the effort that eventually led to the Adoption and Safe Families Act. Signed into law by her husband, she considered the legislation one of her greatest triumphs.

THE GOOD FRIDAY AGREEMENT

In the final year of Bill Clinton's second term, he strengthened his commitment to presenting the United States as a worldwide peacemaker. He saw an opportunity for peace in Northern Ireland. For four decades, Catholic Republicans (seeking a unified Irish republic free of British rule) and Protestant Unionists (committed to Northern Ireland's continued association with the United Kingdom) engaged in vicious fighting and seemingly endless violence. The Irish Republican Army (IRA) was not above acts of terrorism in its pursuit of an independent and unified Ireland. Its associated political party was called Sinn Féin. Clinton—primarily through his envoy, former senator George Mitchell—was able to persuade the leader of Sinn Féin, Gerry Adams, to fight as hard for peace as the IRA had fought for Irish Republicanism.

In the last days of his presidency, Bill Clinton met with British and Irish leaders to encourage progress from their historic peace agreement.

In April 1998, the participants in the talks approved the historic Good Friday Agreement, which authorized a new Catholic-Protestant power-sharing government in Northern Ireland. The agreement also called for the IRA

QUICK FACT

Northern Ireland is variously described as a province or region of the United Kingdom. Following the Irish War of Independence (1919–21), Northern Ireland opted to remain within the United Kingdom, while the twenty-six southern counties formed what would become the Republic of Ireland, which is entirely independent of England.

to disarm. It was a historic peace accord between the Republicans and Unionists that devolved local government responsibilities in Northern Ireland to an elected assembly.

On his last official trip as president in December 2000, Clinton was hailed as a peacemaker in Ireland and Northern Ireland.

CHAPTER 4

BEYOND THE WHITE HOUSE

After leaving the White House in 2001, Bill Clinton remained active in political affairs and was a popular speaker on the lecture circuit. His autobiography, *My Life*, was published in 2004. Later that year, the William J. Clinton Presidential Library and Museum opened in Little Rock, Arkansas.

SENATOR CLINTON

In early 2000, the Clintons bought a house in Chappaqua, New York. Hillary moved there so that she could run for one of New York's seats in the Senate. That fall she became the first First Lady to be elected to public office. Rather than relying on her name and her husband's lingering power and influence in her first year on the job, she humbly accepted her role as a freshman senator. Her fellow senators commented that she was a workhorse, not a show horse.

Hillary's first term as senator was focused on improving the state of New York. Her efforts were needed after the terrorist attacks of September 11, 2001. In New York City, some 2,750 people were killed in the attacks upon the World Trade Center, including more than 400 police officers and firefighters who died on the job while trying to rescue those trapped in and

As a freshman New York senator, Clinton worked to receive federal aid for New York City after the September 11, 2001, attacks.

around the Twin Towers. Clinton was heavily involved in the recovery efforts. She secured funding to rebuild the city and improve security.

As senator, Clinton continued to push for health care reform and remained an advocate for children. She encountered some unhappiness among her more liberal supporters when, in

2002, she voted in support of invading Iraq. As the war, which began in 2003, dragged on for years and became increasingly unpopular, Hillary distanced herself from her vote. She stated, "Obviously, if we knew then what we know now, there wouldn't have been a vote, and I certainly wouldn't have voted that way." She was easily reelected in 2006.

THE CLINTON FOUNDATION

After leaving the White House in 2001, President Clinton built on the legacy of his final years in office by continuing to address global issues with the William J. Clinton Foundation. World leaders identified projects for the former president. Nelson Mandela urged Clinton to fight the HIV

Pictured above in 2007, Clinton visits the construction site for a new hospital in the village of Neno in Malawi, one of the projects supported by his foundation.

and AIDS pandemic and improve global access to care and treatment. So Clinton began the Clinton HIV/AIDS Initiative, now named the Clinton Health Access Initiative (CHAI).

In 2005, after a tsunami in the Indian Ocean had caused widespread death and devastation, Clinton was appointed by United Nations

QUICK FACT

Millions of people have died from AIDS since the 1980s. Scientists have not yet found a cure, but drug therapies now exist that have greatly extended the lives of many AIDS patients.

Secretary-General Kofi Annan to serve as a special envoy for relief efforts.

The Clinton Foundation added more initiatives to its agenda and expanded its reach around the world. The Clinton Climate Initiative focuses on global warming and reducing human impact on the environment. The Clinton Development Initiative helps farmers in Africa receive the assistance they need to lift their families and positively affect their communities. The Clinton Giustra Enterprise Partnership creates economic opportunities in Latin America. In September 2005, the foundation gathered world leaders, interested businessmen,

QUICK FACT

Obesity raises the risk of heart attacks, strokes, and certain cancers.

and other philanthropists to work together and take on issues that others could not or would not. This group has made $73.5 billion in commitments and has affected more than four hundred million people around the world.

In response to Clinton's own experience with heart disease, the foundation teamed with the American Heart Association to form the Alliance for a Healthier Generation. The partnership focused on ending childhood obesity in America. The foundation's health efforts eventually led to the launch of the Clinton Health Matters Initiative in 2012. The initiative promotes healthy lifestyles for people of all ages and works on reducing health disparities among communities.

In addition to the smaller-scale initiatives addressed by the Bill, Hillary & Chelsea Clinton Foundation, the Clinton Global Initiative was launched in 2005 to tackle global issues with world leaders.

Hillary and Chelsea Clinton joined the Clinton Foundation in 2013. The foundation officially changed its name to the Bill, Hillary & Chelsea Clinton Foundation.

First Gentleman?

In 2007, Hillary announced that she would seek the Democratic presidential nomination for 2008. Considered the early front-runner, she spent months locked in a tight contest with Senator Barack Obama. Bill campaigned energetically and enthusiastically for Hillary. Obama eventually secured the nomination and went on to be elected president. He appointed Hillary to serve as secretary of state.

As secretary of state, Hillary Clinton introduced the Quadrennial Diplomacy and Development Review. It was designed to improve the efficiency of the State Department and make sure tax dollars are spent wisely. She also worked hard to repair diplomatic ties with world leaders after the bitter controversies associated with the wars in Iraq and Afghanistan and George W. Bush's "War on Terror." Clinton also championed the Global Hunger and Food Security Initiative that sought to frame the global fight against hunger as a central aspect of U.S. foreign policy. During her years as secretary of state, Clinton sought to balance the military

Though they were rivals during the 2008 primaries, Hillary Clinton supported Obama in his first term as president, then retired to pursue her own interests, including a possible presidential run in 2016.

might of the United States with its capacity to foster economic development, technological advances, and greater respect for human rights worldwide.

Although she lost the nomination for president in 2008, there are hints that she may run for president again in 2016. With her political experience in the White House, U.S. Senate, and State Department, Hillary Clinton just might make Bill Clinton the first "First Gentleman" in U.S. history.

August 19, 1946: Bill Clinton is born.

October 26, 1947: Hillary Rodham is born.

1975: Hillary and Bill Clinton are married.

1978: Bill Clinton wins the election for governor of Arkansas.

1992: Bill Clinton defeats George H. W. Bush to become president of the United States.

1993: The North American Free Trade Agreement (NAFTA) is passed.

1996: Bill Clinton defeats Bob Dole to gain a second term as president of the United States.

1997: The State Children's Health Insurance Program is passed.

1998: The U.S. House of Representatives impeaches Bill Clinton.

1999: The U.S. Senate acquits President Bill Clinton.

2000: Hillary Clinton becomes U.S. senator of New York.

2001: Bill Clinton concludes his second term as president, reenters private life, and founds the Clinton Foundation.

2002: The Clinton Foundation begins the Clinton Health Access Initiative.

2005: The Clinton Global Initiative begins its work.

2006: Hillary Clinton is reelected as U.S. senator of New York.

2007: Hillary Clinton launches her campaign for the presidency of the United States.

2009: Hillary Clinton becomes secretary of state.

2009: Hillary Clinton introduces the Quadrennial Diplomacy and Development Review for the State Department.

2013: Hilary Clinton retires as secretary of state; Hillary and Chelsea Clinton join the Clinton Foundation.

- **The Dalai Lama.** The Dalai Lama is the leader of the main branch of the religion known as Tibetan Buddhism. The fourteenth Dalai Lama travels around the world to promote peace and speak about Tibetans' desire for political independence from China. In 1989, he won the Nobel Peace Prize for his nonviolent work to end Chinese control of Tibet.

- **Bill and Melinda Gates.** Bill Gates, founder and chairman of Microsoft, and his wife, Melinda, created the Bill & Melinda Gates Foundation, the largest charitable foundation in the United States. The foundation's primary focus was on education and global health. By 2006, its endowment was about $30 billion.

- **Nelson Mandela.** Nelson Mandela spent almost thirty years in prison for fighting against apartheid in South Africa. Apartheid was a government policy that separated people of different races and violently suppressed the majority black population. After being freed from prison, Mandela became South Africa's first black president and worked hard to heal the wounds of South Africa's sharply divided society. He died in 2013 and was hailed as a a heroic example of courage, integrity, justice, forgiveness, and peacemaking.

- **Sonia Sotomayor.** Sonia Sotomayor is an American lawyer and judge who became a justice of the U.S. Supreme Court. Sotomayor was the first Hispanic person and the third woman to serve on the Supreme Court.

- **Aung San Suu Kyi.** Aung San Suu Kyi brought international attention to the struggle for human rights in Burma (Myanmar) and fought for democracy. An advocate of nonviolent protest, she was under house arrest in Yangon when she was awarded the 1991 Nobel Peace Prize.

centrist A person with political views that are moderate or middle-of-the-road.

constitution The fundamental rules by which a state and its people are governed.

deferment A temporary exemption from military service.

deficit An excess of spending; what results when more money is spent than is taken in as revenue or is on hand to be spent.

discrimination Unfair treatment of a person or group.

electoral college A group of electors chosen by voters who select the president and vice president of the United States.

freshman A beginner; the first year of an academic program or job.

impromptu Without advance preparation; spontaneous.

legislation The act of making laws by a law-making body, such as the U.S. Congress, or the laws themselves.

preconception A bias or opinion formed ahead of time, before facts are presented or events unfold.

primary An election in which voters select candidates for representative government positions.

quadrennial Occurring every four years.

stagnation The state of having stopped or stalled, with no growth, development, or progress.

stipulation A specific demand within a larger agreement.

welfare Financial assistance given to people in need.

Books

Bausum, Ann. *Our Country's Presidents: All You Need to Know About the Presidents, from George Washington to Barack Obama.* Washington, DC: National Geographic, 2009.

Driscoll, Laura, and Judith V. Wood. *Hillary Clinton: An American Journey.* New York, NY: Grosset & Dunlap, 2008.

Krull, Kathleen, and Amy June Bates. *Hillary Rodham Clinton: Dreams Taking Flight.* New York, NY: Simon & Schuster Books for Young Readers, 2008.

Smithsonian Institution. *Presidents FYI.* New York, NY: HarperCollins Children's Books, 2008.

Venezia, Mike. *Bill Clinton: Forty-Second President, 1993-2001.* New York, NY: Children's Press/Scholastic, 2008.

Wells-Cole, Catherine. *Political Profiles: Hillary Clinton.* Greensboro, NC: Morgan Reynolds, 2008.

Websites

Because of the changing nature of Internet links, Rosen Publishing has developed an online list of websites related to the subject of this book. This site is updated regularly. Please use this link to access this list:

http://www.rosenlinks.com/mad/clint